gets you through

C000183482

KS2 MATHS
SATs SUCCESS
PRACTICE TEST PAPERS

Ages 10–11

KS2 MATHS SATs

2 complete tests

PRACTICE TEST PAPERS

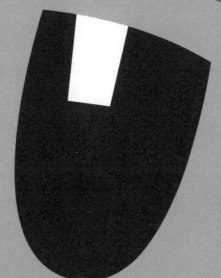

TOM HALL

Contents

Introduction and instructions

How these tests will help your child

This book is made up of two complete sets of practice test papers. Each set contains similar test papers to those that your child will take in maths at the end of Year 6. They can be used any time throughout the year to provide practice for the Key Stage 2 tests.

The results of both sets of papers will provide a good idea of the strengths and weaknesses of your child.

Administering the tests

- Provide your child with a quiet environment where they can complete each test undisturbed.
- Provide your child with a pen or pencil, ruler, eraser and protractor. A calculator is **not** allowed.
- The amount of time given for each paper varies, so remind your child at the start of each one how long they have and give them access to a clock or watch.
- You should only read the instructions out to your child, not the actual questions.
- Although handwriting is not assessed, remind your child that their answers should be clear.
- Advise your child that if they are unable to do one of the questions they should go on to the next one and come back to it later, if they have time. If they finish before the end, they should go back and check their work.

Paper 1: arithmetic

- Answers are worth 1 or 2 marks, with a total number of 40 marks. Long multiplication and long division questions are worth 2 marks each. A mark may be awarded for showing the correct method.
- Your child will have **30 minutes** to answer the questions as quickly and carefully as they can.
- Encourage your child to look at the number of marks after each question to help them find out how much detail is required in their answer.
- Where questions are expressed as common fractions, the answers should be given as common fractions. All other answers should be given as whole or decimal numbers.

Paper 2 and Paper 3: reasoning

- Answers are worth 1, 2 or 3 marks, with a total number of 35 marks. A mark may be awarded for showing the correct method in specific questions where there is a method box.
- Your child will have **40 minutes** to answer the questions as quickly and carefully as they can.
- Encourage your child to look at the number of marks after each question to help them find out how much detail is required in their answer.
- If your child needs to do some working out, advise them that they can use the space around the question.

© 2018 Letts Educational, an imprint of HarperCollinsPublishers Ltd – not to be photocopied.

Marking the practice test papers

The answers and mark scheme have been provided to enable you to check how your child has performed. Fill in the marks that your child achieved for each part of the tests.

Please note: these tests are **only a guide** to the standard or mark your child can achieve and cannot guarantee the same is achieved during the Key Stage 2 tests, as the mark needed to achieve the expected standard varies from year to year.

	Set A	Set B
Paper 1: arithmetic	/ 40	/ 40
Paper 2: reasoning	/ 35	/ 35
Paper 3: reasoning	/ 35	/ 35
Total	/ 110	/ 110

The scores achieved on these practice test papers will help to show if your child is working at the expected standard in maths:
35–54 = working towards the expected standard
55–74 = working at the expected standard
75–110 = working above the expected standard.

When an area of weakness has been identified, it is useful to go over it and to look at similar types of questions with your child. Sometimes your child will be familiar with the subject matter but might not understand what the question is asking. This will become apparent when talking to your child.

Shared marking and target setting

Engaging your child in the marking process will help them to develop a greater understanding of the tests and, more importantly, provide them with some ownership of their learning. They will be able to see more clearly how and why certain areas have been identified for them to target for improvement.

Top tips for your child

Don't make silly mistakes. Make sure you emphasise to your child the importance of reading the question. Easy marks can be picked up by just doing as the question asks.

Make answers clearly legible. If your child has made a mistake, encourage them to put a cross through it and write the correct answer clearly next to it. Try to encourage your child to use an eraser as little as possible.

Don't panic! These practice test papers, and indeed the end of Key Stage 2 tests, are meant to provide a guide to the standard a child has attained. They are not the be-all and end-all, as children are assessed regularly throughout the school year. Explain to your child that there is no need to worry if they cannot do a question – tell them to go on to the next question and come back to the problematic question later if they have time.

 © 2018 Letts Educational, an imprint of HarperCollinsPublishers Ltd – not to be photocopied.

Key Stage 2

Maths

Paper 1: arithmetic

You **may not** use a calculator to answer any questions in this test paper.

Time:

You have **30 minutes** to complete this test paper.

Maximum mark	Actual mark
40	....

First name	
Last name	

Date of birth	Day		Month		Year	

© 2018 Letts Educational, an imprint of HarperCollinsPublishers Ltd – not to be photocopied.

1   43 × 5 =

1 mark

2   574 + 56 =

1 mark

3   1,234 + 100 =

1 mark

 © 2018 Letts Educational, an imprint of HarperCollinsPublishers Ltd – not to be photocopied.

4

$\dfrac{2}{5} + \dfrac{2}{5} =$

1 mark

5

= 9,999 – 1,000

1 mark

6

868 + 130 =

1 mark

7

607 × 3 =

1 mark

8

8.1 ÷ 10 =

1 mark

9

316 + 86 =

1 mark

© 2018 Letts Educational, an imprint of HarperCollinsPublishers Ltd – not to be photocopied.

10 $5^2 =$

1 mark

11 $492 \div 3 =$

1 mark

12 ☐ $= \dfrac{9}{10} - \dfrac{1}{5}$

1 mark

© 2018 Letts Educational, an imprint of HarperCollinsPublishers Ltd – not to be photocopied.

13 10 − 15 =

1 mark

14 $\dfrac{1}{2} + \dfrac{2}{5} =$

1 mark

15 $\dfrac{1}{3} \times 24 =$

1 mark

© 2018 Letts Educational, an imprint of HarperCollinsPublishers Ltd – not to be photocopied.

16 $\frac{1}{2} \div 4 =$

1 mark

17 $\boxed{} = 0.6 \times 4$

1 mark

18 50% of 2,500 =

1 mark

19

$50 - 5 \times 10 =$

1 mark

20

$5{,}725 + 3{,}750 =$

1 mark

21

$5{,}804 - 5{,}075 =$

1 mark

© 2018 Letts Educational, an imprint of HarperCollinsPublishers Ltd – not to be photocopied.

22 47.32 – 15.44 =

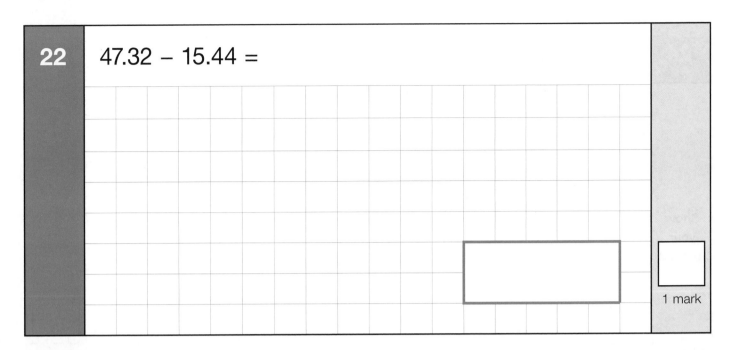

1 mark

23 486.48 – 39.57 =

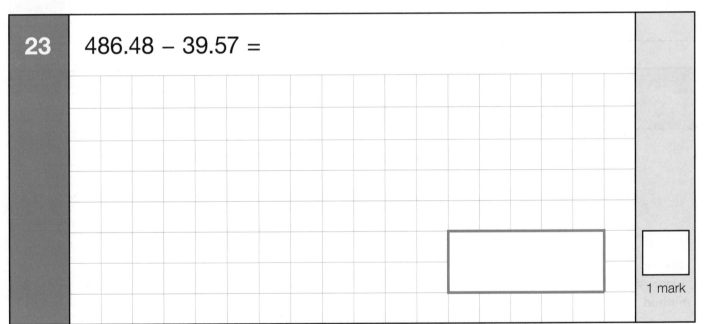

1 mark

© 2018 Letts Educational, an imprint of HarperCollinsPublishers Ltd – not to be photocopied.

24

```
      3  4
×     2  6
```

Show your method

2 marks

25

```
2  3 | 5  5  2
```

Show your method

2 marks

© 2018 Letts Educational, an imprint of HarperCollinsPublishers Ltd – not to be photocopied.

26 30.75 × 100 =

1 mark

27 $\frac{3}{4} + \frac{4}{12} =$

1 mark

28 78.7 − 65.88 =

1 mark

© 2018 Letts Educational, an imprint of HarperCollinsPublishers Ltd – not to be photocopied.

29 | $\boxed{}$ = 65 ÷ 100

1 mark

30 | 50.806 − 32.661 =

1 mark

© 2018 Letts Educational, an imprint of HarperCollinsPublishers Ltd – not to be photocopied.

31

Show your method

$$\begin{array}{r} 5\ 7\ 3 \\ \times\quad 4\ 5 \\ \hline \end{array}$$

2 marks

32

$\dfrac{3}{5} \div 4 =$

1 mark

33

3 5 | 8 7 5

Show your method

2 marks

34

$40 \times 1\frac{1}{2} =$

1 mark

© 2018 Letts Educational, an imprint of HarperCollinsPublishers Ltd – not to be photocopied.

35 $\dfrac{1}{3} \times \dfrac{1}{5} =$

1 mark

36 $56.77 - 5.777 =$

1 mark

SET
A

Maths

PAPER 2

Key Stage 2

Maths

Paper 2: reasoning

You **may not** use a calculator to answer any questions in this test paper.

Time:

You have **40 minutes** to complete this test paper.

Maximum mark	Actual mark
35	

First name	
Last name	

Date of birth	Day		Month		Year	

© 2018 Letts Educational, an imprint of HarperCollinsPublishers Ltd – not to be photocopied.

1 This is part of a number square.

Circle all the numbers that have a remainder of 1 when divided by 4.

12	13	14	15	16
22	23	24	25	26
32	33	34	35	36
42	43	44	45	46
52	53	54	55	56

2 marks

2 Draw a pentagon with a pair of parallel lines.

Use a ruler.

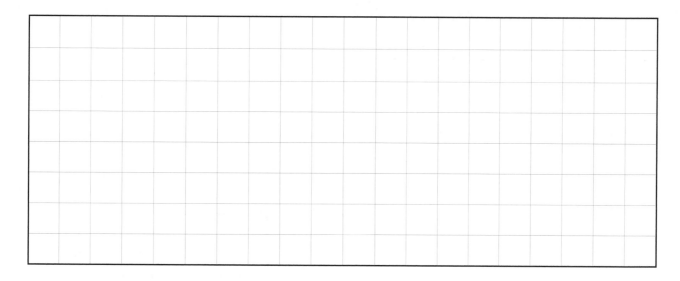

2 marks

© 2018 Letts Educational, an imprint of HarperCollinsPublishers Ltd – not to be photocopied.

3 Ellie and Rosie each buy one pizza.

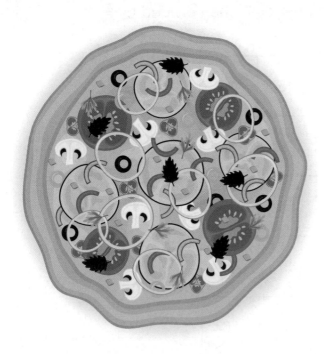 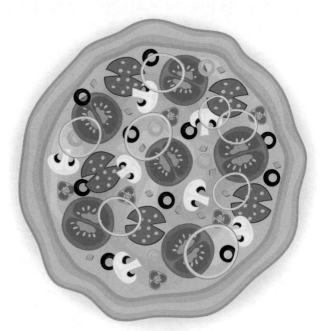

Ellie eats $\frac{5}{8}$ of her pizza.

Rosie eats $\frac{7}{8}$ of her pizza.

What fraction of one pizza is left?

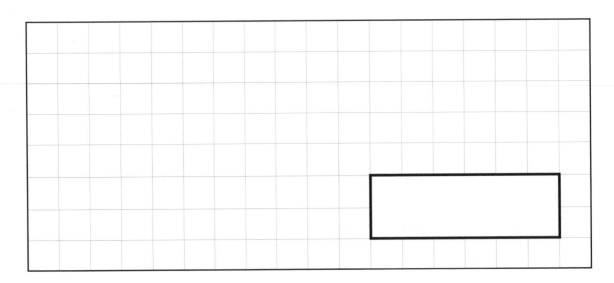

1 mark

© 2018 Letts Educational, an imprint of HarperCollinsPublishers Ltd – not to be photocopied.

4 Tick (✔) the two numbers that have a difference of 1000.

32,658 ☐

33,758 ☐

33,768 ☐

34,758 ☐

43,858 ☐

1 mark

5 Write the missing digits in this calculation.

```
    5 ☐ 4 ☐
+   ☐ 5 ☐ 4
_____
  1 2 6 0 0
```

1 mark

6 Calculate the perimeter of this shape.

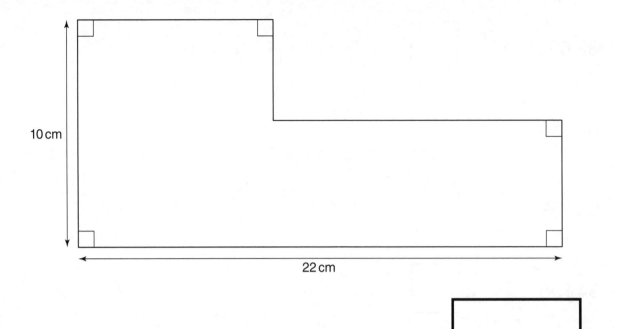

10 cm

22 cm

cm

1 mark

7 A number squared and a number cubed both equal 64.

Find the numbers.

$\boxed{}^2 = 64 = \boxed{}^3$

1 mark

8 Four hundred and sixty thousand, three hundred and five

Write this number in digits.

1 mark

 © 2018 Letts Educational, an imprint of HarperCollinsPublishers Ltd – not to be photocopied.

9 Reflect the shape in the mirror line.

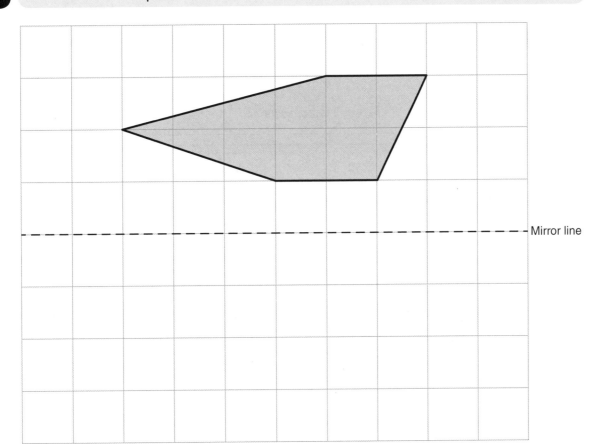

Mirror line

1 mark

10 This table gives approximate conversions between kilograms and pounds.

kilograms	pounds
1	2.2
2	4.4
4	8.8
8	17.6
16	35.2

Use the table to convert 7 kilograms into pounds.

pounds

1 mark

Use the table to convert 22 pounds into kilograms.

kg

1 mark

© 2018 Letts Educational, an imprint of HarperCollinsPublishers Ltd – not to be photocopied.

11 This is the plan of a football ground which has seats for 48,139 spectators.

The number of seats is shown for three of the stands.

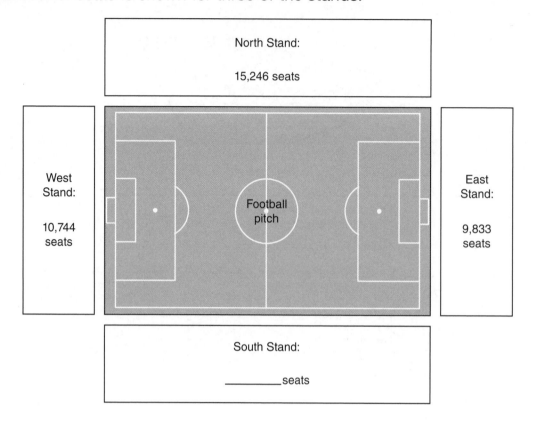

North Stand:

15,246 seats

West Stand:

10,744 seats

Football pitch

East Stand:

9,833 seats

South Stand:

_____ seats

How many seats are there in the South Stand?

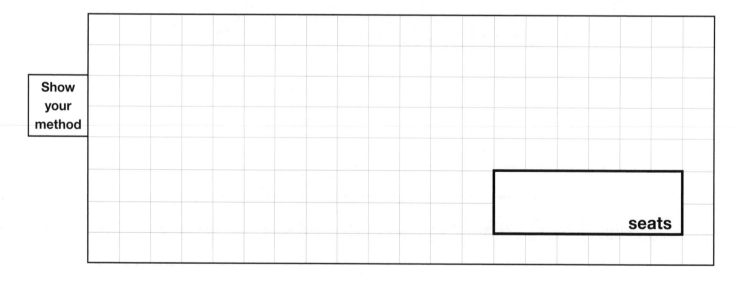

Show your method

seats

2 marks

© 2018 Letts Educational, an imprint of HarperCollinsPublishers Ltd – not to be photocopied.

12 Tick (✔) the largest number.

56.276   56.093   56.239   56.198   56.273

[ ]   [ ]   [ ]   [ ]   [ ]

1 mark

13 Tom has a collection of football cards.

Tom has 5 coloured cards to every 3 black and white cards.

He has 36 black and white cards.

Tom gives $\frac{1}{5}$ of his coloured cards to Jack.

How many cards does Tom give to Jack?

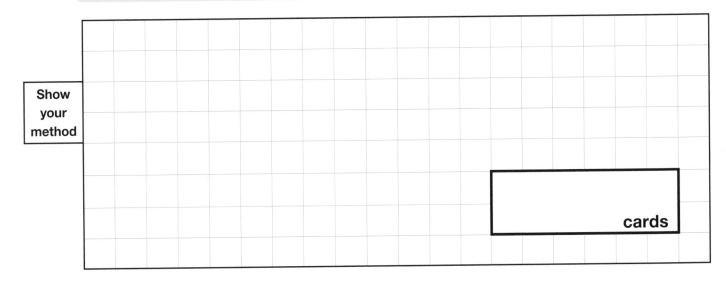

Show your method

cards

2 marks

© 2018 Letts Educational, an imprint of HarperCollinsPublishers Ltd – not to be photocopied.

14 330 ÷ 8 =

Give your answer as a decimal.

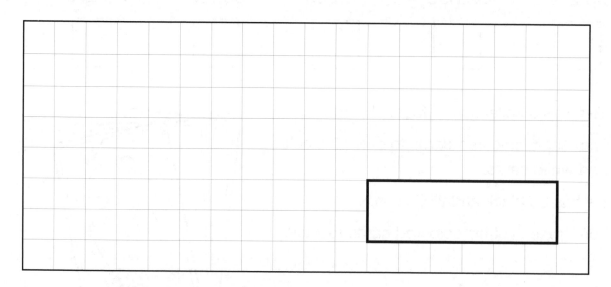

1 mark

15 Oakview School has 460 pupils.

40% are girls.

Sea Lane School has 240 pupils.

60% are girls.

How many more girls are there at Oakview School?

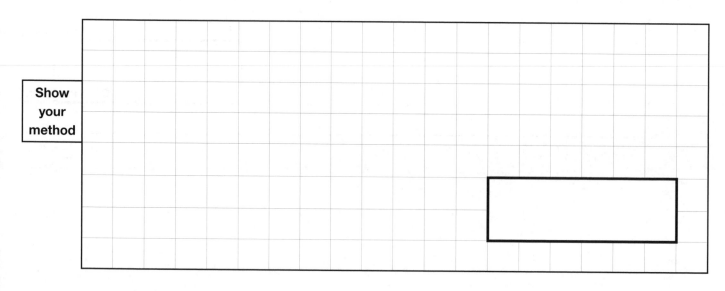

Show your method

3 marks

  © 2018 Letts Educational, an imprint of HarperCollinsPublishers Ltd – not to be photocopied.

16 Find the value of $5a - 2b$, when $a = 5$ and $b = 7$.

1 mark

Find the value of $5a + 2b$, when $a = 7$ and $b = 5$.

1 mark

17 Here are two equations with missing numbers.

□ + △ = 18

□ − △ = 6

Work out the value of the missing numbers.

□ =

△ =

2 marks

18 Here are four containers holding some water.

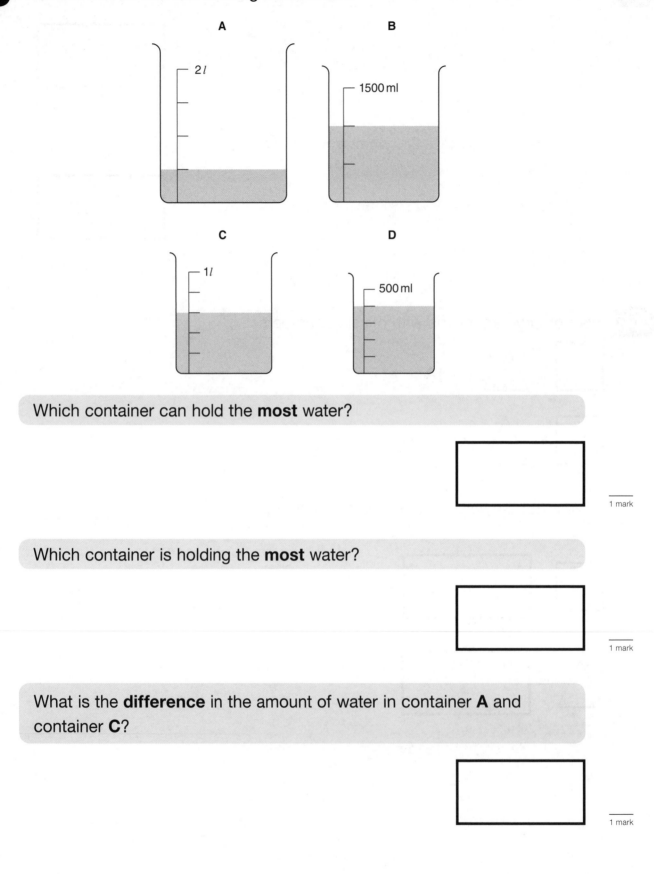

Which container can hold the **most** water?

1 mark

Which container is holding the **most** water?

1 mark

What is the **difference** in the amount of water in container **A** and container **C**?

1 mark

© 2018 Letts Educational, an imprint of HarperCollinsPublishers Ltd – not to be photocopied.

19 Tick (✔) the circle with a radius drawn as a dashed line.

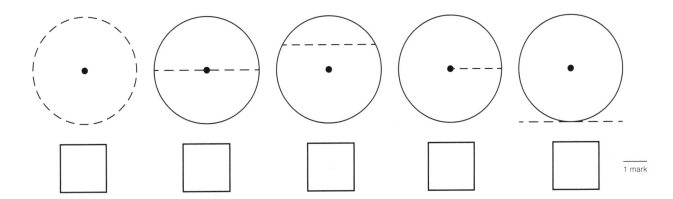

☐   ☐   ☐   ☐   ☐

1 mark

20 Here is a set of numbers.

7   15   24   30   48   53

Which two numbers are **common multiples** of 3 and 4?

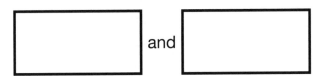 and ☐

1 mark

Which two numbers are **common factors** of 60?

☐ and ☐

1 mark

Which two numbers are **prime numbers**?

☐ and ☐

1 mark

21 Sally wants to go on holiday to Spain.

She compares the mean temperatures for UK and Spain.

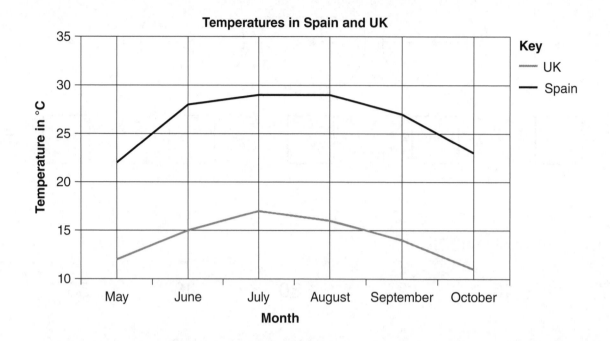

How much **warmer** was it in Spain than in UK in September?

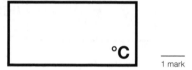

1 mark

Sally wants to go to Spain when it is closest to 25°C.

Which **two** months could Sally choose?

_____

1 mark

© 2018 Letts Educational, an imprint of HarperCollinsPublishers Ltd – not to be photocopied.

Key Stage 2

Maths

Paper 3: reasoning

You **may not** use a calculator to answer any questions in this test paper.

Time:

You have **40 minutes** to complete this test paper.

Maximum mark	Actual mark
35	....

First name	
Last name	

Date of birth	Day		Month		Year	

© 2018 Letts Educational, an imprint of HarperCollinsPublishers Ltd – not to be photocopied.

1 What number is shown by this abacus?

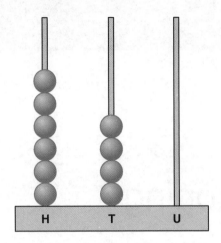

1 mark

2 Find the missing number.

$9 \times \boxed{} = 72 \div 2$

1 mark

3 What time is shown on this clock?

1 mark

© 2018 Letts Educational, an imprint of HarperCollinsPublishers Ltd – not to be photocopied.

4 Part of this shape is missing.

The dotted line is a line of symmetry.

Complete the shape.

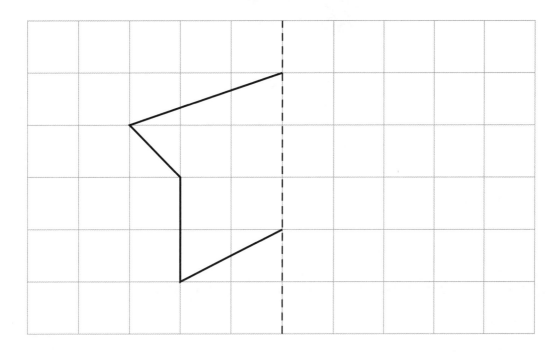

1 mark

Draw the line of symmetry on this shape.

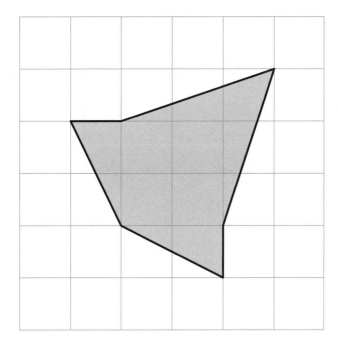

1 mark

5 Chloe has 217 minutes left on her phone.

She uses 83 minutes.

She gets another 350 minutes.

How many minutes does Chloe have on her phone now?

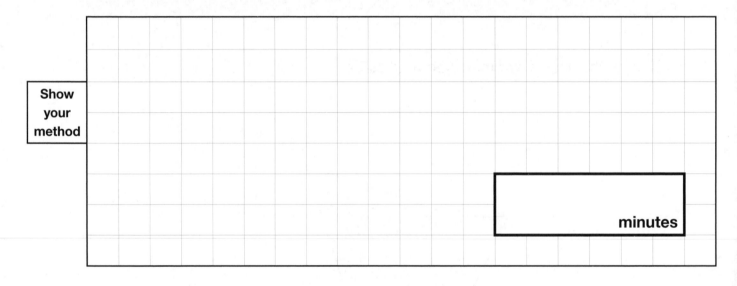

Show your method

minutes

2 marks

© 2018 Letts Educational, an imprint of HarperCollinsPublishers Ltd – not to be photocopied.

6 Tom buys 5 identical books for a total of £26.

What is the cost of each book?

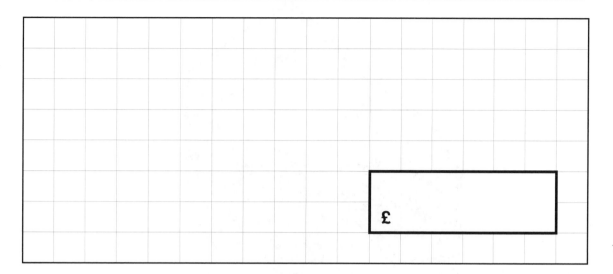

£

1 mark

7 1 inch is about 2.5 centimetres.

How many centimetres is 12 inches?

cm

1 mark

There are 12 inches in 1 foot.

There are 3 feet in 1 yard.

Is 1 yard shorter or longer than 1 metre? Explain how you know.

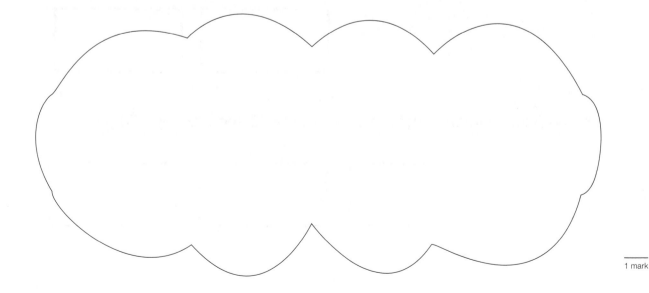

1 mark

© 2018 Letts Educational, an imprint of HarperCollinsPublishers Ltd – not to be photocopied.

8 The temperature outside a greenhouse is −4°C.

The temperature inside the greenhouse is 4°C.

What is the **difference** between the two temperatures?

°C

1 mark

9 Two prime numbers total 31.

What are the two numbers?

1 mark

List the prime numbers that are greater than 40 and less than 50.

1 mark

 © 2018 Letts Educational, an imprint of HarperCollinsPublishers Ltd – not to be photocopied.

10 Manisha has 24 counters.

- $\frac{1}{4}$ of the counters are red.

- $\frac{1}{3}$ of the counters are blue.

- $\frac{3}{8}$ of the counters are green.

The rest of the counters are yellow.

How many yellow counters are there?

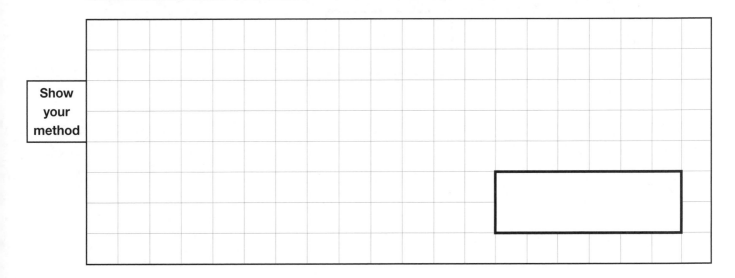

Show
your
method

2 marks

© 2018 Letts Educational, an imprint of HarperCollinsPublishers Ltd – not to be photocopied.

11 878,421 – 319,875 =

Round each number in this calculation to the nearest hundred thousand to work out an estimated answer.

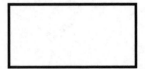

1 mark

12 For each number, give the value of the digit 8.

7,376,548

8,065,913

5,682,790

7,368,514

2 marks

© 2018 Letts Educational, an imprint of HarperCollinsPublishers Ltd – not to be photocopied.

13 An aeroplane is flying at a height of 8,000 m.

The outside temperature is −45°C.

Inside the aeroplane the temperature is 18°C.

What is the **difference** between the two temperatures?

°C

1 mark

14 The population of a city is 275,386.

- 54,895 are aged 65 and over.

- 143,706 are aged 18 to 64.

How many are aged under 18?

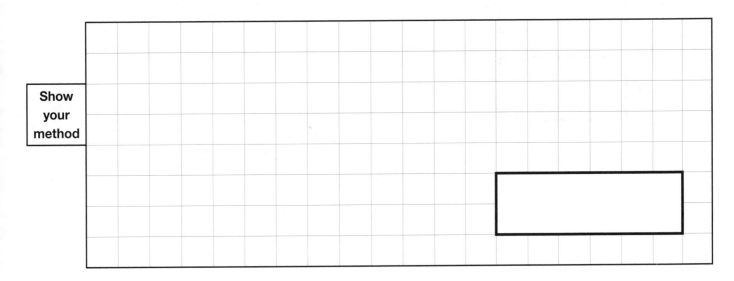

Show your method

2 marks

15 Draw a line from each fraction to the common factor used to simplify it.

$\dfrac{24}{30}$ 3

$\dfrac{21}{30}$ 4

$\dfrac{28}{32}$ 5

$\dfrac{20}{25}$ 6

2 marks

16 These two triangles are the same shape but different sizes.

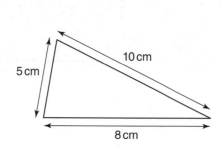 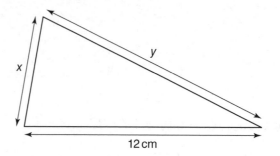

Work out the lengths of the sides *x* and *y*.

$X = $ [ ] cm

1 mark

$y = $ [ ] cm

1 mark

© 2018 Letts Educational, an imprint of HarperCollinsPublishers Ltd – not to be photocopied.

17 Write these masses in order, **heaviest** first.

2.5 kg   200 g   2.05 kg   2,550 g   2.005 kg

☐   ☐   ☐   ☐   ☐

1 mark

18 Tick (✔) each box if the fact about the drawn shape is true.

	has at least 1 pair of parallel sides	has at least 1 pair of perpendicular sides
Right-angled triangle	☐	☐
Rectangle	☐	☐
Parallelogram	☐	☐

3 marks

© 2018 Letts Educational, an imprint of HarperCollinsPublishers Ltd – not to be photocopied.

19 Teachers asked 120 children where they would like to go on a school visit.

This pie chart shows where they chose to go.

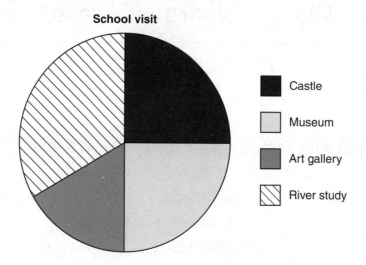

School visit

Estimate how many children chose to visit the castle.

1 mark

40 children chose the river study.

What size angle at the centre of the pie chart is needed to show the river study?

1 mark

Half the children chose either the river study or the art gallery.

How many children chose to visit the art gallery?

1 mark

© 2018 Letts Educational, an imprint of HarperCollinsPublishers Ltd – not to be photocopied.

20 Abi sat 6 tests.

Her mean score was 45.

How many marks did Abi score **altogether**?

1 mark

21 A formula to find the perimeter, *P*, of a rectangle is

$$P = 2l + 2w, \text{ where } l = \text{length and } w = \text{width}$$

Work out the length of a rectangle that has a perimeter of 80 cm and a width of 10 cm.

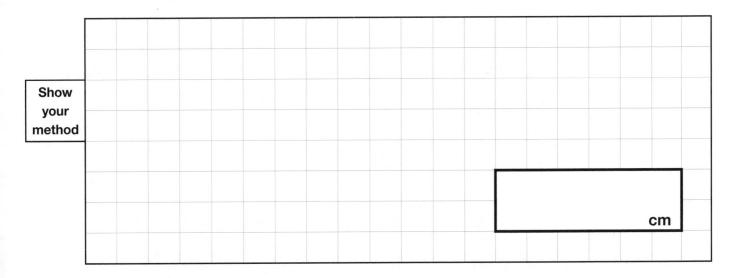

Show
your
method

cm

2 marks

© 2018 Letts Educational, an imprint of HarperCollinsPublishers Ltd – not to be photocopied.

Key Stage 2

Maths

Paper 1: arithmetic

You **may not** use a calculator to answer any questions in this test paper.

Time:

You have **30 minutes** to complete this test paper.

Maximum mark	Actual mark
40	....

First name	
Last name	

Date of birth	Day		Month		Year	

© 2018 Letts Educational, an imprint of HarperCollinsPublishers Ltd – not to be photocopied.

1   40 ÷ 5 =

1 mark

2   828 − 102 =

1 mark

3 $\frac{7}{8} - \frac{4}{8} =$

1 mark

© 2018 Letts Educational, an imprint of HarperCollinsPublishers Ltd – not to be photocopied.

4 $\frac{1}{2} \times 30 =$

1 mark

5   [   ] $= 888 + 1,000$

1 mark

6 $855 + 477 =$

1 mark

© 2018 Letts Educational, an imprint of HarperCollinsPublishers Ltd – not to be photocopied.

7 | 765 ÷ 5 =

1 mark

8 | 0.6 × 100 =

1 mark

9 | 2,705 + 7,808 =

1 mark

© 2018 Letts Educational, an imprint of HarperCollinsPublishers Ltd – not to be photocopied.

10

$\boxed{} = 3^3$

1 mark

11

$4{,}088 \times 6 =$

1 mark

12

$12.45 - 8.49 =$

1 mark

© 2018 Letts Educational, an imprint of HarperCollinsPublishers Ltd – not to be photocopied.

13 $0.03 \times 6 =$

1 mark

14 $\frac{1}{2} - \frac{1}{10} =$

1 mark

15 $4 - 12 =$

1 mark

© 2018 Letts Educational, an imprint of HarperCollinsPublishers Ltd – not to be photocopied.

16

$\boxed{}$ = 325.8 + 4.67

1 mark

17

80,000 − 8,000 =

1 mark

18

$\frac{1}{10} \div 2 =$

1 mark

 © 2018 Letts Educational, an imprint of HarperCollinsPublishers Ltd – not to be photocopied.

19   9,360 − 745 =

1 mark

20   23.9 + 4.76 =

1 mark

21 $5\frac{3}{4} - \frac{3}{8} =$

1 mark

© 2018 Letts Educational, an imprint of HarperCollinsPublishers Ltd – not to be photocopied.

22 20 × 30 × 40 =

1 mark

23 30% of 3,000 =

1 mark

24 75 ÷ 1,000 =

1 mark

© 2018 Letts Educational, an imprint of HarperCollinsPublishers Ltd – not to be photocopied.

25 654.23 – 40.8 =

1 mark

26

Show your method

```
    1 8 2
  ×   6 2
```

2 marks

27

$100 \times 2\frac{1}{2} =$

1 mark

28

$2\ 2\ \overline{)\ 7\ 0\ 4}$

Show your method

2 marks

© 2018 Letts Educational, an imprint of HarperCollinsPublishers Ltd – not to be photocopied.

29

40 + 10 × 2 =

1 mark

30

Show your method

7 1 ⟌ 1 4 9 1

2 marks

31

$4\dfrac{2}{3} - 3\dfrac{3}{5} =$

1 mark

32

Show your method

$$\begin{array}{r} 3\ 0\ 7\ 4 \\ \times\quad\ \ 3\ 5 \\ \hline \end{array}$$

2 marks

 © 2018 Letts Educational, an imprint of HarperCollinsPublishers Ltd – not to be photocopied.

33   4,000,000 – 400,000 =

1 mark

34   78.357 – 6.05 =

1 mark

35 $\dfrac{3}{5} \times 40 =$

1 mark

© 2018 Letts Educational, an imprint of HarperCollinsPublishers Ltd – not to be photocopied.

36 $\frac{2}{3} \div 2 =$

1 mark

© 2018 Letts Educational, an imprint of HarperCollinsPublishers Ltd – not to be photocopied.

Key Stage 2

Maths

Paper 2: reasoning

You **may not** use a calculator to answer any questions in this test paper.

Time:

You have **40 minutes** to complete this test paper.

Maximum mark	Actual mark
35	....

First name	
Last name	

Date of birth	Day		Month		Year	

© 2018 Letts Educational, an imprint of HarperCollinsPublishers Ltd – not to be photocopied.

1   Tick (✔) the right angles in this shape.

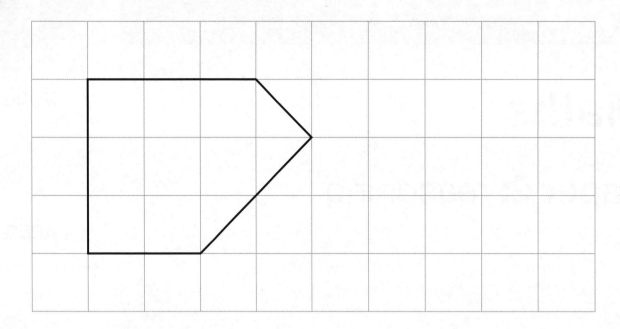

1 mark

2   Here are some counters.

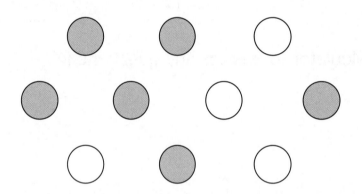

What fraction of the counters are grey?

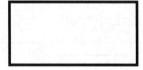

1 mark

62

© 2018 Letts Educational, an imprint of HarperCollinsPublishers Ltd – not to be photocopied.

3 Dev read 26 books in a school year.

He drew a graph to show how many books he read each term.

Complete the bar for Term 3.

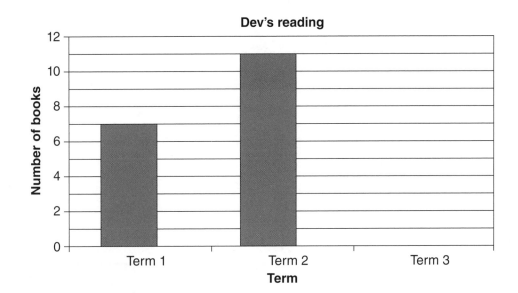

1 mark

4 A train has 8 coaches.

Each coach has 72 seats.

The ticket collector says, 'I know 70 × 8 = 560'

What must he add to 560 to find how many seats there are in the train **altogether**?

1 mark

5 Find the missing number.

$64 × 24 = (64 × 20) + (64 × \boxed{}) = 1,536$

1 mark

© 2018 Letts Educational, an imprint of HarperCollinsPublishers Ltd – not to be photocopied.

6 A square is drawn on an empty grid.

The coordinates of three vertices are marked.

What are the coordinates of the fourth vertex?

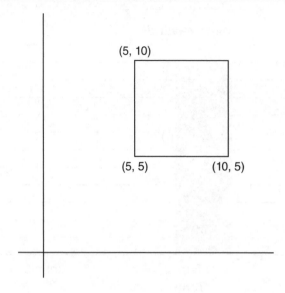

$$\boxed{\left(\underline{\quad} , \underline{\quad} \right)}$$

1 mark

7 A shop has a special offer.

> Special offer!
>
> Buy 3 tins of soup and get 1 free

Obi pays for 12 tins of soup.

How many tins does Obi get?

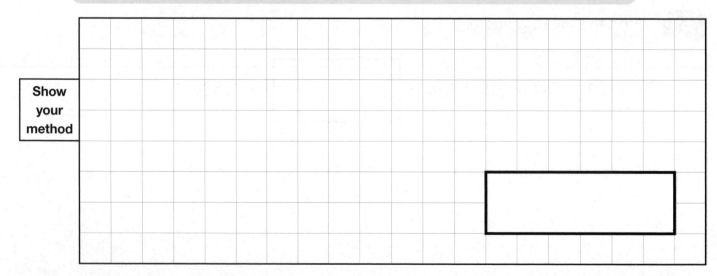

Show your method

2 marks

© 2018 Letts Educational, an imprint of HarperCollinsPublishers Ltd – not to be photocopied.

8 Max makes some concrete for a path.

For a path 8 metres long Max needs:

- 200 kg of cement

- 600 kg of sand

- 600 kg of stone

What weight of stone will he need for a path 20 metres long?

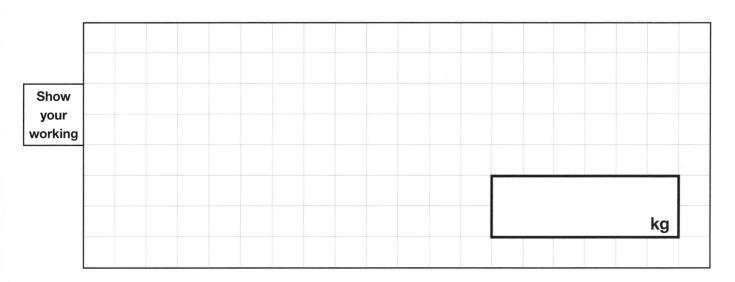

Show
your
working

kg

2 marks

© 2018 Letts Educational, an imprint of HarperCollinsPublishers Ltd – not to be photocopied.

9 Calculate the missing number.

$$56 \times 9 = \boxed{} + 4$$

1 mark

Calculate the missing number.

$$56 + 64 = 3 \times 4 \times \boxed{}$$

2 marks

10 Here are some digit cards.

Use the digit cards to complete this equation.

Use each card only once.

$$\boxed{}\boxed{}\boxed{} \div 100 = \boxed{} . \boxed{}\boxed{}$$

1 mark

11

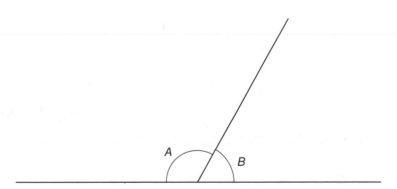

What is the **total** of angle *A* and angle *B*?

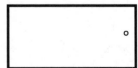

°

1 mark

© 2018 Letts Educational, an imprint of HarperCollinsPublishers Ltd – not to be photocopied.

12 Josh wants to buy tickets for a concert.

He needs 9 adult tickets and 3 child tickets.

CONCERT

Tickets

Adult: £24.70

Child: £18.50

Group of 12:   £249.99

How much will Josh save if he buys the group ticket?

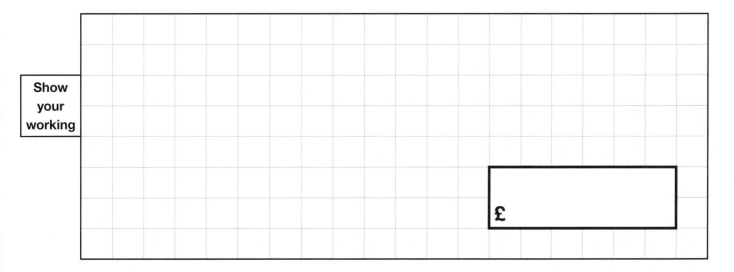

Show your working

£

3 marks

13 Here are two fair triangular spinners.

Each spinner is spun once and the numbers added to give a total.

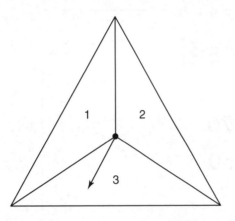 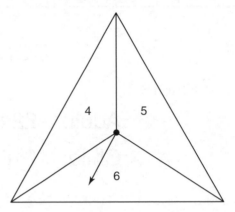

List the totals that can be made.

  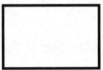 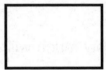

2 marks

14 This sequence decreases in equal steps.

Find the missing numbers.

| 6 | −3 | | | −30 |

2 marks

© 2018 Letts Educational, an imprint of HarperCollinsPublishers Ltd – not to be photocopied.

15 Josef is thinking of a six-digit number.

Josef's number has:

- three hundred thousand

- seven hundred

- forty thousand

All the other digits are 6.

Use these facts to complete the number.

[ ][ ][ ],[ ][ ][ ]

1 mark

16 This table shows the temperatures in five cities.

City	London	Belfast	Manchester	Cardiff	Glasgow
Temperature	4°C	0°C	–3°C	–1°C	–5°C

What is the **difference** between the temperatures in Manchester and Cardiff?

°C

1 mark

What is the **difference** between the warmest and coldest temperatures?

°C

1 mark

© 2018 Letts Educational, an imprint of HarperCollinsPublishers Ltd – not to be photocopied.

17   Find the missing numerators in these equations.

$$\frac{3}{4} = \frac{\boxed{}}{24}$$

$$\frac{5}{6} = \frac{\boxed{}}{24}$$

$$\frac{3}{8} = \frac{\boxed{}}{24}$$

$$\frac{2}{3} = \frac{\boxed{}}{24}$$

2 marks

18   What could the missing digits be?

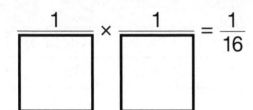

$$\frac{1}{\boxed{}} \times \frac{1}{\boxed{}} = \frac{1}{16}$$

1 mark

$$\frac{\boxed{}}{\boxed{}} \times \frac{\boxed{}}{\boxed{}} = \frac{2}{8} = \frac{1}{4}$$

1 mark

© 2018 Letts Educational, an imprint of HarperCollinsPublishers Ltd – not to be photocopied.

19 Dev and Sam share £45.

Dev takes half the amount Sam takes.

How much do they each take?

Dev takes £ [ ]

Sam takes £ [ ]

1 mark

20 This rectangle has an area of 24 cm².

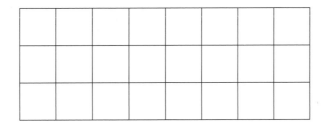

Write the lengths and widths of two different rectangles that also have an area of 24 cm².

length [ ] cm and width [ ] cm

1 mark

length [ ] cm and width [ ] cm

1 mark

© 2018 Letts Educational, an imprint of HarperCollinsPublishers Ltd – not to be photocopied.

21 Angles *x* and *y* are equal.

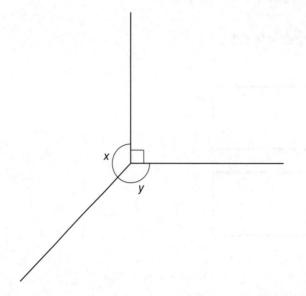

Calculate angle *x*.

X = [   ] °

1 mark

 © 2018 Letts Educational, an imprint of HarperCollinsPublishers Ltd – not to be photocopied.

22 Ben describes two shapes.

Name each shape.

My first shape has four
right angles and two pairs
of sides of 10 cm and 5 cm.

_____

1 mark

My second shape has four
angles (two that are 120° and
two that are 60°) and two pairs
of sides that are 10 cm and 5 cm.

_____

1 mark

© 2018 Letts Educational, an imprint of HarperCollinsPublishers Ltd – not to be photocopied.

Key Stage 2

Maths

Paper 3: reasoning

You **may not** use a calculator to answer any questions in this test paper.

Time:

You have **40 minutes** to complete this test paper.

Maximum mark	Actual mark
35	

First name	
Last name	

Date of birth	Day		Month		Year	

© 2018 Letts Educational, an imprint of HarperCollinsPublishers Ltd – not to be photocopied.

1 Here are some digit cards:

| 3 | 4 | 5 | 6 | 7 |

Use the digits to make this correct.

Use each card once.

```
[   ]  [   ]  [   ]
[ + ]  [   ]  [   ]
_____
[ 6 ]  [ 0 ]  [ 1 ]
```

2 marks

2 This is a rectangle.

Tick (✔) **two** correct statements.

The two bold lines are perpendicular. ☐

The bold and thin lines are perpendicular. ☐

The two bold lines are parallel. ☐

The bold and thin lines are parallel. ☐

2 marks

© 2018 Letts Educational, an imprint of HarperCollinsPublishers Ltd – not to be photocopied.

3 Dom sells computer games.

This pictogram shows the number of computer games he sold one week.

Computer Game Sales

⊙ stands for four computer games

Sunday	⊙ ⊙ ⊙ ⊙
Monday	⊙ ◖
Tuesday	⊙ ◔
Wednesday	⊙
Thursday	⊙ ⊙ ⊙
Friday	⊙ ⊙ ⊙ ◜
Saturday	⊙ ⊙ ⊙ ⊙

How many computer games did Dom sell in total on Friday and Saturday?

games

1 mark

How many more games did Dom sell on Sunday than on Monday?

games

1 mark

4 Tick (✔) all the shapes that have $\frac{2}{3}$ shaded.

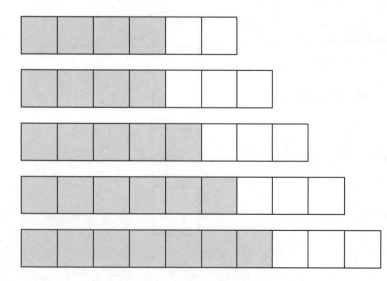

2 marks

© 2018 Letts Educational, an imprint of HarperCollinsPublishers Ltd – not to be photocopied.

5 Ned has a 10 kg bag of potatoes.

He uses 2.3 kg of the potatoes one day.

He uses 1,600 g of the potatoes on the next day.

What is the weight of potatoes left?

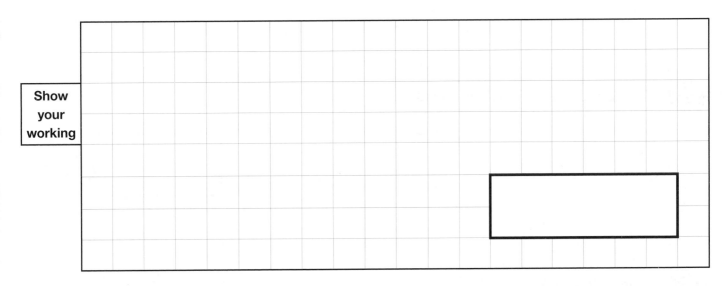

Show
your
working

2 marks

© 2018 Letts Educational, an imprint of HarperCollinsPublishers Ltd – not to be photocopied.

6 Translate the shape 7 squares right and 3 squares down.

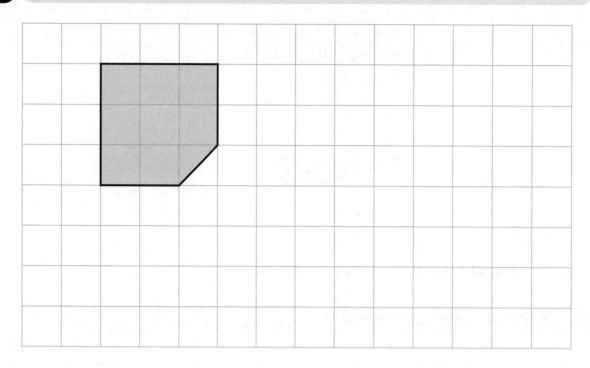

2 marks

7 Write the year MMXXII in digits.

1 mark

8 Circle the number that is both:

- a factor of 36

- a multiple of 12

9   18   24   36   72

1 mark

© 2018 Letts Educational, an imprint of HarperCollinsPublishers Ltd – not to be photocopied.

9 Round **196,704**

to the nearest ten

to the nearest thousand

to the nearest hundred thousand

2 marks

10 Complete this table of equivalent fractions, decimals and percentages.

Fraction		Decimal		Percentage
$\frac{65}{100}$	=		=	
	=	0.8	=	
	=		=	7%

2 marks

11 Write the following as digits.

one million, thirty-seven thousand, six hundred and four

1 mark

12 Here are three digit cards.

Use each card to complete the missing digits in these sentences.

Use each card only once.

 is a prime number.

 is a common multiple of 3 and 7.

 is a common factor of 62 and 93.

2 marks

© 2018 Letts Educational, an imprint of HarperCollinsPublishers Ltd – not to be photocopied.

13 Find the missing digit.

$$\frac{2}{3} < \frac{\boxed{}}{12} < \frac{5}{6}$$

1 mark

14 Tara thinks of a number, n.

She adds 12 to the number and then multiplies the answer by 3.

Tick (✔) the expression that shows this.

$3n + 12$

$3(n + 12)$

$3 \times 12 \times n$

$36 + n$ $\boxed{}$

$n(3 + 12)$ $\boxed{}$

1 mark

© 2018 Letts Educational, an imprint of HarperCollinsPublishers Ltd – not to be photocopied.

15 Measure the marked angle using a protractor.

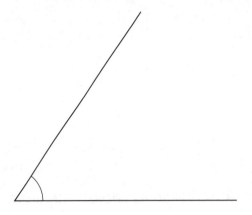

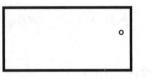

1 mark

16 Sam sat two maths tests.

These were his scores:

Paper 1: $\frac{14}{20}$

Paper 2: $\frac{18}{25}$

Change Sam's fraction scores to percentage scores.

Paper 1:  %

Paper 2:  %

2 marks

© 2018 Letts Educational, an imprint of HarperCollinsPublishers Ltd – not to be photocopied.

17 This pie chart shows the sports chosen by 80 children.

Here are some facts about the pie chart:

- 30 children chose tennis.

- $\frac{1}{4}$ of the children chose football.

- The same number of children chose gymnastics as chose rugby.

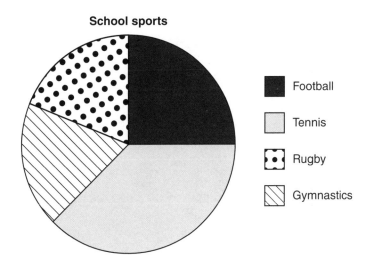

School sports

Football
Tennis
Rugby
Gymnastics

How many children chose rugby?

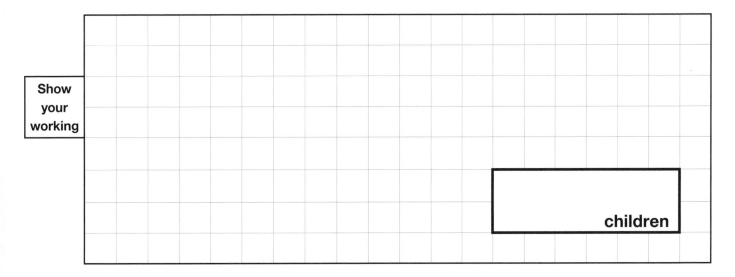

Show your working

children

2 marks

© 2018 Letts Educational, an imprint of HarperCollinsPublishers Ltd – not to be photocopied.

18 Tick (✔) the number with 7 as the hundredths digit.

6.497 ☐

64.97 ☐

649.7 ☐

6,497 ☐

64,970 ☐

649,700 ☐

1 mark

© 2018 Letts Educational, an imprint of HarperCollinsPublishers Ltd – not to be photocopied.

19   Work out the area of this triangle.

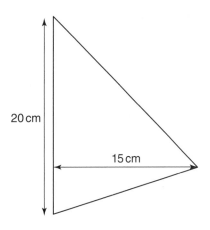

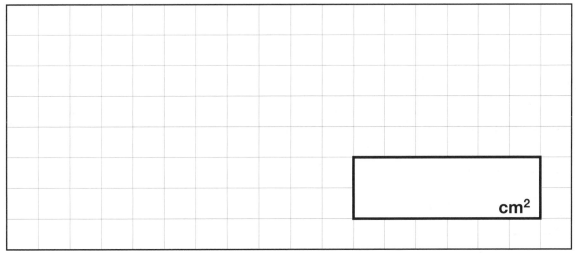

cm²

Work out the length of this parallelogram.

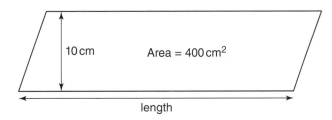

Area = 400 cm²

length

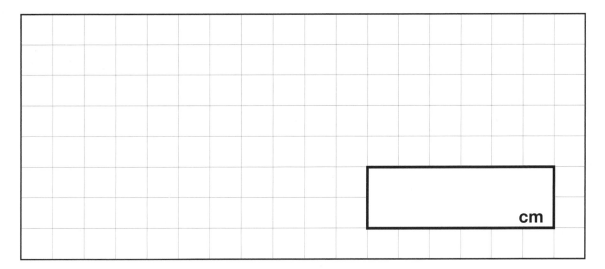

cm

© 2018 Letts Educational, an imprint of HarperCollinsPublishers Ltd – not to be photocopied.

20 The dots, A to F, can be joined to make a straight line.

The dots are drawn at regular intervals.

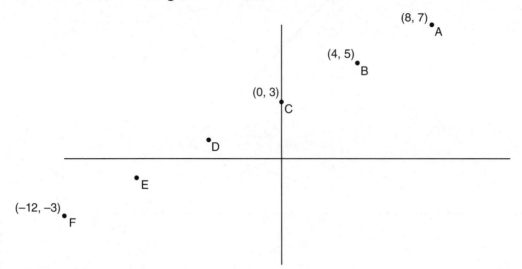

Some dots have coordinates.

What are the coordinates of dots D and E?

D = $\left(\underline{\quad}, \underline{\quad}\right)$

E = $\left(\underline{\quad}, \underline{\quad}\right)$

2 marks

© 2018 Letts Educational, an imprint of HarperCollinsPublishers Ltd – not to be photocopied.

21 Tickets to an amusement park cost £17.50 each.

There is a special offer. Eight tickets can be bought for £110.

How much cheaper is **each** ticket with the special offer?

<table>
<tr><td>Show your method</td><td></td></tr>
</table>

£

2 marks

© 2018 Letts Educational, an imprint of HarperCollinsPublishers Ltd – not to be photocopied.

Answers

Set A Paper 1

#	Answer	Mark
1.	215	(1 mark)
2.	630	(1 mark)
3.	1,334	(1 mark)
4.	$\frac{4}{5}$ (Accept equivalent fractions)	(1 mark)
5.	8,999	(1 mark)
6.	998	(1 mark)
7.	1,821	(1 mark)
8.	0.81	(1 mark)
9.	402	(1 mark)
10.	25	(1 mark)
11.	164	(1 mark)
12.	$\frac{7}{10}$ (Accept equivalent fractions)	(1 mark)
13.	−5 (Do not accept 5−)	(1 mark)
14.	$\frac{9}{10}$ (Accept equivalent fractions)	(1 mark)
15.	8	(1 mark)
16.	$\frac{1}{8}$ (Accept equivalent fractions)	(1 mark)
17.	2.4	(1 mark)
18.	1,250	(1 mark)
19.	0	(1 mark)
20.	9,475	(1 mark)
21.	729	(1 mark)
22.	31.88	(1 mark)
23.	446.91	(1 mark)

24.

```
          3 4
    ×     2 6
    ---------
        2 0 4
      6 8 0
    ---------
      8 8 4
```

(2 marks for correct answer. Award 1 mark for using long multiplication with no more than one error but wrong answer given. Do not award any marks if the 0 for multiplying by a ten is missing. Do not award any marks if no final answer is given.)

25.

```
            2 4
    2 3 ) 5 5 2
          4 6
          -----
            9 2
            9 2
          -----
            0
```

(2 marks for correct answer. Award 1 mark for using long division with no more than one error but wrong answer given. Do not award any marks if no final answer is given.)

#	Answer	Mark
26.	3,075	(1 mark)
27.	$1\frac{1}{12}$ (Accept equivalent fractions)	(1 mark)
28.	12.82	(1 mark)
29.	0.65	(1 mark)
30.	18.145	(1 mark)

© 2018 Letts Educational, an imprint of HarperCollinsPublishers Ltd – not to be photocopied.

31.

		5	7	3
	×		4	5
	2	8	6	5
2	2	9	2	0
2	5	7	8	5

(2 marks for correct answer. Award 1 mark for using long multiplication with no more than one error but wrong answer given. Do not award any marks if the 0 for multiplying by a ten is missing. Do not award any marks if no final answer is given.)

32. $\frac{3}{20}$ (Accept equivalent fractions)

(1 mark)

33.

			2	5	
3	5	8	7	5	
		7	0		
		1	7	5	
		1	7	5	
				0	

(2 marks for correct answer. Award 1 mark for using long division with no more than one error but wrong answer given. Do not award any marks if no final answer is given.)

34. 60 **(1 mark)**

35. $\frac{1}{15}$ **(1 mark)**

36. 50.993 **(1 mark)**

Set A Paper 2

1. 13, 25, 33, 45 and 53 circled only.
(2 marks: 1 mark for three answers circled)

2. **(2 marks: 1 mark for a shape with five sides; 1 mark for a pair of parallel lines)**

3. $\frac{1}{2}$ (Accept $\frac{4}{8}$ or other equivalent fractions) **(1 mark)**

4. 33,758 and 34,758 ticked only.
(1 mark: 1 mark for both correct answers)

5.

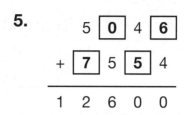

(1 mark: all correct for 1 mark)

6. 64 cm **(1 mark)**

7. 8, 4 **(1 mark)**

8. 460,305 **(1 mark)**

9.

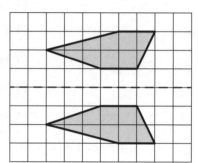

(Accept lines drawn to within 2 mm of vertices) **(1 mark)**

10. 15.4 pounds **(1 mark)**
10 kg **(1 mark)**

11. 12,316
(2 marks for correct answer. Award 1 mark for correct working with wrong answer.)

12. 56.276 ticked only. **(1 mark)**

13. 12
(2 marks for correct answer. Award 1 mark for correct working with wrong answer.)

14. 41.25 **(1 mark)**

15. 40
(3 marks for correct answer. Award 1 mark for finding 40% of 460 = 184 or 1 mark for finding 60% of 240 = 144 or 1 mark for a correct subtraction of the answers even if the percentages are incorrect.)

© 2018 Letts Educational, an imprint of HarperCollinsPublishers Ltd – not to be photocopied.

16. 11 **(1 mark)**

45 **(1 mark)**

17. ☐ = 12, △ = 6

(2 marks for correct answer. Award 1 mark for ☐ = 6, △ = 12)

18. A **(1 mark)**

B **(1 mark)**

100 ml or 0.1 l **(1 mark)**

19. 4th shape ticked only. **(1 mark)**

20. 24 and 48 **(1 mark)**

15 and 30 **(1 mark)**

7 and 53 **(1 mark)**

21. 13°C (Accept +/− 1°C) **(1 mark)**

September and October **(1 mark)**

Set A Paper 3

1. 640 **(1 mark)**

2. 4 **(1 mark)**

3. 7:20 (Accept 7:20 am, 7:20 pm, 19:20, 20 past 7) **(1 mark)**

4.

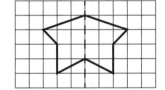

(Accept lines drawn to within 2 mm of vertices. Ignore lines that are not straight.) **(1 mark)**

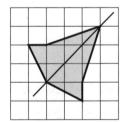

(Accept lines drawn within 2 mm of the vertices.) **(1 mark)**

5. 217 − 83 = 134;

134 + 350 = 484 minutes

(2 marks for correct answer. Award 1 mark for correct working, but wrong answer given.)

6. £5.20 (Do not accept 5.2) **(1 mark)**

7. 30 cm **(1 mark)**

Explanation should show that there are approximately 90 cm (3 × 30 cm) in 1 yard and 90 cm < 100 cm **(1 mark)**

8. 8°C **(1 mark)**

9. 2 and 29 (Accept answers in either order) **(1 mark)**

41 43 47 **(1 mark)**

10. $(\frac{1}{4} \times 24) + (\frac{1}{3} \times 24) + (\frac{3}{8} \times 24) = 23$;

6 + 8 + 9 = 23; 24 − 23 = 1

(2 marks for correct answer. Award 1 mark for correct working, but wrong answer given.)

11. 600,000 (Do not accept 558,546)

(1 mark)

12. 8 or eight units or eight ones

8,000,000 or eight million

80,000 or eighty thousand or eight ten thousands

8,000 or eight thousand

(2 marks: 2 marks for four correct answers, 1 mark for two or three correct answers)

13. 63°C **(1 mark)**

14. 275,386 − (54,895 + 143,706) = 76,785

(2 marks for correct answer. Award 1 mark for correct working, but wrong answer given.)

15.

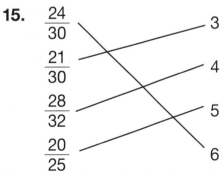

(2 marks: 2 marks for four lines correctly drawn, 1 mark for two or three lines correctly drawn)

16. $x = 7.5\,\text{cm}$ **(1 mark)**

$y = 15\,\text{cm}$ **(1 mark)**

17. 2,550 g   2.5 kg   2.05 kg

2.005 kg   200 g (Accept units that have been converted correctly, e.g. 2,550 g   2,500 g   2,050 g   2005 g   200 g) **(1 mark)**

18. Right-angled triangle ☐ ☑

Rectangle ☑ ☑

Parallelogram ☑ ☐

(3 marks: 1 mark for each shape)

19. 30 (Accept +/− 1) **(1 mark)**

120° **(1 mark)**

20 **(1 mark)**

20. 270 **(1 mark)**

21. $80 = 2l + 2 \times 10$; $80 = 2l + 20$;

$60 = 2l$; $60 \div 2 = l = 30\,\text{cm}$

(2 marks for correct answer. Award 1 mark for correct working, but wrong answer given.)

Set B Paper 1

1. 8 **(1 mark)**

2. 726 **(1 mark)**

3. $\frac{3}{8}$ (Accept equivalent fractions) **(1 mark)**

4. 15 **(1 mark)**

5. 1,888 **(1 mark)**

6. 1,332 **(1 mark)**

7. 153 **(1 mark)**

8. 60 **(1 mark)**

9. 10,513 **(1 mark)**

10. 27 **(1 mark)**

11. 24,528 **(1 mark)**

12. 3.96 **(1 mark)**

13. 0.18 **(1 mark)**

14. $\frac{2}{5}$ (Accept $\frac{4}{10}$ and other equivalent fractions) **(1 mark)**

15. −8 (Do not accept 8−) **(1 mark)**

16. 330.47 **(1 mark)**

17. 72,000 **(1 mark)**

18. $\frac{1}{20}$ (Accept equivalent fractions) **(1 mark)**

19. 8,615 **(1 mark)**

20. 28.66 **(1 mark)**

21. $5\frac{3}{8}$ (Accept equivalent fractions. Accept $\frac{43}{8}$) **(1 mark)**

22. 24,000 **(1 mark)**

23. 900 **(1 mark)**

24. 0.075 **(1 mark)**

25. 613.43 **(1 mark)**

26.

			1	8	2
		×		6	2
			3	6	4
	1	0	9	2	0
	1	1	2	8	4

(2 marks for correct answer. Award 1 mark for using long multiplication with no more than one error but wrong answer given. Do not award any marks if the 0 for multiplying by a ten is missing. Do not award any marks if no final answer is given.)

27. 250 **(1 mark)**

28.

				3	2
	2	2	7	0	4
			6	6	
				4	4
				4	4
					0

(2 marks for correct answer. Award 1 mark for using long division with no more than one error but wrong answer given. Do not award any marks if no final answer is given.)

29. 60 **(1 mark)**

© 2018 Letts Educational, an imprint of HarperCollinsPublishers Ltd – not to be photocopied.

30.

```
            2 1
   7 1 | 1 4 9 1
         1 4 2
             7 1
             7 1
               0
```

(2 marks for correct answer. Award 1 mark for using long division with no more than one error but wrong answer given. Do not award any marks if no final answer is given.)

31. $1\frac{1}{15}$ (Accept equivalent fractions)

(1 mark)

32.

```
        3 0 7 4
   ×        3 5
     1 5 3 7 0
     9 2 2 2 0
   1 0 7 5 9 0
```

(2 marks for correct answer. Award 1 mark for using long multiplication with no more than one error but wrong answer given. Do not award any marks if the 0 for multiplying by a ten is missing. Do not award any marks if no final answer is given.)

33. 3,600,000 **(1 mark)**

34. 72.307 **(1 mark)**

35. 24 **(1 mark)**

36. $\frac{1}{3}$ (Accept equivalent fractions)

(1 mark)

Set B Paper 2

1.

(1 mark: all three right angles needed for 1 mark)

2. $\frac{3}{5}$ (Accept equivalent fractions, e.g. $\frac{6}{10}$. Accept 0.6 or 60%)

(1 mark)

3. A bar or line drawn to show 8

(1 mark)

4. 16 or 2 × 8 **(1 mark)**

5. 4 **(1 mark)**

6. (10, 10) **(1 mark)**

7. 12 ÷ 3 = 4; 12 + 4 = 16 tins

(2 marks for correct answer. Award 1 mark for correct working, but wrong answer given.)

8. 20 ÷ 8 = 2.5; 600 × 2.5 = 1500 kg

(2 marks for correct answer. Award 1 mark for correct working, but wrong answer given.)

9. 500
10

(2 marks for correct answer. Award 1 mark for sight of: 56 + 64 = 120 or 3 × 4 = 12 or 120 ÷ 12)

10. Accept any correct answer, e.g.
456 ÷ 100 = 4.56; 465 ÷ 100 = 4.65;
546 ÷ 100 = 5.46; 564 ÷ 100 = 5.64;
645 ÷ 100 = 6.45; 654 ÷ 100 = 6.54

(1 mark)

11. 180° **(1 mark)**

12. £27.81

(3 marks for correct answer. Award 1 mark for a correct method of finding the cost of 9 adult and 3 child tickets with a wrong answer and award 1 mark for a correct method of finding the difference between the cost of the individual tickets and the group ticket with a wrong answer.)

13. 5   6   7   8   9

(2 marks: 2 marks for five correct answers, 1 mark for three or four correct answers)

14. −12   −21

(2 marks: 1 mark for each correct answer)

15. 346,766 **(1 mark)**

16. 2°C (1 mark)

9°C (1 mark)

17. $\dfrac{3}{4}$ = $\dfrac{18}{24}$

$\dfrac{3}{8}$ = $\dfrac{9}{24}$

$\dfrac{5}{6}$ = $\dfrac{20}{24}$

$\dfrac{2}{3}$ = $\dfrac{16}{24}$

(2 marks: 2 marks for four correct answers, 1 mark for two or three correct answers)

18. Accept $\dfrac{1}{2} \times \dfrac{1}{8}$ or $\dfrac{1}{8} \times \dfrac{1}{2}$

or $\dfrac{1}{4} \times \dfrac{1}{4}$ or $\dfrac{1}{1} \times \dfrac{1}{16}$ **(1 mark)**

$\dfrac{1}{2} \times \dfrac{2}{4}$ or $\dfrac{1}{1} \times \dfrac{2}{8}$ (Accept for either calculation numerators or denominators reversed) **(1 mark)**

19. Dev takes £15

Sam takes £30 **(1 mark)**

20. Possible answers are:

length 24 cm width 1 cm

length 12 cm width 2 cm

length 6 cm width 4 cm

(Accept lengths and widths reversed. Accept fractions and decimals if correct, e.g. 48 cm × 0.5 cm. Do not accept length 3 cm, width 8 cm)

(2 marks: 1 mark for each pair of correct answers)

21. 135° **(1 mark)**

22. rectangle (Accept oblong) **(1 mark)**

parallelogram **(1 mark)**

Set B Paper 3

1. Possible answers: 567 + 34, 564 + 37, 537 + 64, 534 + 67

(2 marks: 1 mark for correct placing of 7 and 4 in the units column)

2. 2nd and 3rd boxes ticked only.

(2 marks: 1 mark for each correct box ticked)

3. 29 games **(1 mark)**

10 games **(1 mark)**

4. 1st and 4th shapes ticked only.

(2 marks: 1 mark for each correct box ticked)

5. 10 − (2.3 + 1.6) = 6.1 kg or 10,000 − (2,300 + 1,600) = 6,100 g (Accept 6.1 kg or 6100 g. Units must be correct, e.g. do not accept 6.1 g or 6,100 kg. Accept 6,100 or 6.1 without units.)

(2 marks for correct answer. Award 1 mark for correct working, but wrong answer given.)

6.

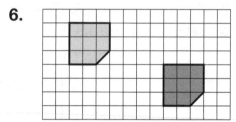

(2 marks: 2 marks for drawing as shown; 1 mark for correctly orientated and sized shape translated 7 units right or 3 units down)

7. 2022 **(1 mark)**

8. 36 circled only. **(1 mark)**

9. 196,700

197,000

200,000

(2 marks: 2 marks for three correct, 1 mark for two correct)

© 2018 Letts Educational, an imprint of HarperCollinsPublishers Ltd – not to be photocopied.

10.

Fraction		Decimal		Percentage
$\frac{65}{100}$	=	0.65	=	65%
$\frac{4}{5}$ or equivalent	=	0.8	=	80%
$\frac{7}{100}$	=	0.07	=	7%

(2 marks: 2 marks for six correct answers, 1 mark for four or five correct answers)

11. 1,037,604 (Accept misplaced commas) **(1 mark)**

12. 53
42
31
(2 marks: 2 marks for three correct answers, 1 mark for two correct answers)

13. 9 **(1 mark)**

14. 2nd box ticked only. **(1 mark)**

15. 55° (Accept angles within 2°) **(1 mark)**

16. Paper 1   70%
Paper 2   72%   **(2 marks)**

17. $\dfrac{80 - (\frac{1}{4} \times 80 + 30)}{2} = 15$ children
(2 marks for correct answer. Award 1 mark for correct working, but wrong answer given.)

18. 2nd box ticked only. **(1 mark)**

19. 150 cm^2 **(1 mark)**
40 cm **(1 mark)**

20. D   (–4, 1)
E   (–8, –1)
(2 marks: 1 mark for each coordinate)

21. £17.50 – (£110 ÷ 8) = £17.50 – £13.75
= £3.75
(2 marks for correct answer. Award 1 mark for correct working, but wrong answer given.)

© 2018 Letts Educational, an imprint of HarperCollinsPublishers Ltd – not to be photocopied.

© 2018 Letts Educational, an imprint of HarperCollinsPublishers Ltd – not to be photocopied.

'Down to Earth' Strafing Aces of the Eighth Air Force